Rebuilding Lives Through Bankruptcy

How to Save Your House, Save Your Car,
Save Your Cash, Save your Marriage,
Save Your Family

By: William A. Grafton, Esq.
Kelly A. Grafton, Esq.
Grafton Firm, LLC

AF701156

Published by Grafton Firm, LLC
Baltimore, Maryland

Printed in the United States of America
ISBN-13: 978-0692786376
ISBN-10: 0692786376

To obtain bulk quantities of this book for educational use, seminars, fundraising, or sales promotions, contact:

William A. Grafton
Grafton Firm, LLC
(410) 870-9315
www.mdbankruptcyfirm.com
www.graftonfirm.com
wgrafton@graftonfirm.com

Contents

Why We're Here

William Grafton, Esq.

When I started law school in the year 2000, I knew one thing. I was going to be financially stable. I wasn't going to have to worry about bills the way my parents worried. I wasn't going to have to cut corners, make my own clothes, stretch food, or go without the way my parents and I did growing up. Let's just say, I had no idea what my future had in store for me.

When I graduated law school in 2003, there was one firm that stood out to me. It wasn't the high-powered litigation firm that I thought I'd wind up with. It wasn't working with a District Attorney's office as a stepping stone to bigger and better things. No, it was a small bankruptcy firm. I started the day I got my bar exam results and two weeks later was figuratively thrown to the wolves. I had my own office and my own staff and family after family coming to me for help in bringing them stability. I loved it. I was the lone attorney working an enormous case load with a staff that trained me almost as much as I trained them. Here I was at 25 years old, helping people twice or more my age. There was one thing I was sure of – I would never be in that position myself.

Wrong.

Two years into my brilliant career disaster literally struck. Hurricane Katrina destroyed everything I owned. My home was washed into the sea along with everything I owned except for about a week's worth of casual clothing. My office was mostly spared and for the next 3 months I lived there, seeing clients late into the night and on weekends. I wasn't the only one who had lost it all, my clients had gone from bad to worse and new clients, people who never would have considered bankruptcy were coming to see me. Suddenly they owned concrete slabs where homes had once stood and still owed massive mortgages. The insurance they thought was their surety against disaster suddenly decided that Hurricanes weren't floods and weren't wind-born storms, so they weren't covered.

After 3 grueling months, with health concerns starting to mount due to constant exposure to mold and overwork, I decided I needed a change of scenery. So, with little fanfare, I packed up my meager belongings and moved to Texas. I wasn't licensed to practice law in Texas yet, so I worked a lot of different types of jobs. I sold timeshares, delivered chicken wings, was a paralegal, built and sold litigation databases to law firms. I was broke, late on my bills, and could barely afford the cost of activating my law license in Texas. My credit score was just about as low as it could get.

When I got my license a job was immediately waiting for me. I started off supervising a small segment of a national law firm who specialized in helping people get out of debt. Within a couple of months I was asked to step in and oversee their Bankruptcy Division. I was training lawyers around the country on Bankruptcy. I was able to repay most of my creditors and settled the rest for less than what I owed. I saw my credit score slowly improving. It occurred to me that at the firm I had left and the firm I was with, that getting people out of debt was only the beginning of what they need. What do you do when the debt is gone? How do you rebuild your credit?

I left that firm in 2013 to join my wife Kelly in this firm. We aren't trying to be the biggest bankruptcy firm in Baltimore. We just want to be the firm that provides the best service at a reasonable price. We want to be the people you can turn to when you need us and we'll still be there when your case is done. We are here to help you begin the rebuilding process.

We are a family firm and we aim to treat every client like part of the family.

Kelly Grafton, Esq.

When I was a freshman in high school, my father lost his job unexpectedly. We were in Disney World on a family trip over Christmas. My parents had saved, cut coupons, and scoured the phone book for discounts. My dad was a Project Manager for a bowling company. He oversaw the building of new bowling allies, billiards halls, and kids' party places. While working on a new center in Orlando, he snuck over to Disney to plan our ultimate vacation. It was the greatest week of my childhood. I saw my parents enjoy spending time with each other and my older brother and I reconnected after years of sibling rivalry and fighting.

There's nothing like "The Happiest Place on Earth" to bring a family together ...

...And, there's nothing like job loss, debt, and financial stress to tear a family apart.

The day we got home from our dream vacation, my father got a call to meet his boss the next day in a conference center at a hotel. He knew something was wrong. I remember sitting with him while he explained his fears. His company of 25 years, the company where his father worked for his entire career, had been bought. Layoffs were coming. The new company had brought in a younger, cheaper version of my father. My father knew this hotel conference room meant the end of his career. He was right. What he didn't know was that this conference room also meant the end of our happy family.

My father was a well-educated, white collar worker with years of experience in project management, contract negotiation, and sales. He was a very marketable candidate. Yet, it took him FOUR YEARS TO FIND A JOB. And, that new job was as an hourly furniture salesman at a discount store.

While my father was unemployed, my mom worked multiple jobs, I took after school jobs, and the bills mounted. Credit cards were maxed out and the financial stress took its toll on my family. My parents fought… a lot. And, my father spiraled down the deep pit of depression. By the time my father found that furniture job, my mother had filed for divorce and I had moved out. My brother and I weren't speaking.

My father ultimately filed for bankruptcy, but the damage was already done. He found a better job, but in the meantime he lost his wife of 25 years, his family, his friends, and his pride.

I didn't set out to be a bankruptcy attorney. I began my career as a corporate litigator in the biggest law firm in the world. After 5 years there, I got caught up in a period of layoffs, just like my father. I never appreciated what my father went through during those years until I faced them myself. Suddenly, I wanted to bury my head and wallow in depression just like he did. But, I would not lose my family too. Instead, I founded my own firm. My husband,

William, who had been practicing bankruptcy law his entire career joined me and taught me all he knew about rescuing families from debt.

Although running a family law firm is challenging and stressful, I take great pride in the fact that we are securing our own future while helping families secure theirs. Seeing the relief on the face of a client who was drowning in debt before meeting us is far more fulfilling than helping a global corporation with a contract dispute.

William and I are writing this book to help other families decide if bankruptcy is right for them and to get answers, not myths. Bankruptcy is not a bad word, it is not shameful. But, it's also not a fix-all solution for every family. Bankruptcy may not have saved my family, but I wish my parents had read a book like this or visited someone like William before it was too late. Simply knowing what options were out there might have made the difference.

Bankruptcy Basics

Chapter 7 Versus Chapter 13

You've probably heard about people "filing for Chapter 7" or "filing for Chapter 13". What does this mean? Well, simply put, the "Chapter" is the chapter of the bankruptcy laws where the bankruptcy rules come from. There is a type of bankruptcy outlined in Chapter 7 of the bankruptcy laws that has certain rules, and another in Chapter 13 with different rules.

Both of these are options for people to have certain debts discharged, which means the debts are excused, written off, or forgiven, but, there are important differences. For example, a Chapter 13 bankruptcy is a voluntary filing that can be withdrawn, a Chapter 7 cannot. Also, Chapter 13 plans usually require repayment of some portion of your debt, but Chapter 7 bankruptcies do not.

Knowing which option is best for you is an art. There are a lot of rules, qualifications, calculations, and strategic decisions that go into determining which bankruptcy option is right for you.

Things we think about to determine which option is best for you:

1. What is your mix of debt? How much is secured debt and how much is unsecured debt?
2. What is your total household income and how many people live in your house?

3. Do you own your home (do you own it alone or with someone else)? How much equity do you have?
4. Do you have other valuable assets (cars, jewelry, furs, electronics, collectibles, boats, etc.)?
5. How much is your total debt?
6. Are you behind on your house or car payments and want to keep the car or house?
7. Do you owe back taxes?
8. Would you benefit from a "cramdown" – reducing the principal (and sometimes interest rate) of a secured loan?
9. Have you had a recent bankruptcy discharge in either Chapter 7 or Chapter 13?
10. Do you owe back child or spousal support that you need time to pay?

While it's good to do your homework and look into all of the options available, remember that a skilled attorney can help you fully understand the pros and cons of each option. At the same time, don't let someone force you into a certain type of bankruptcy.

Chapter 13 bankruptcies are longer and usually generate more attorneys' fees, so beware of an attorney that recommends a Chapter 13 bankruptcy to all of his clients. There are many reasons why a Chapter 13 bankruptcy might be right for you, but make sure you and your attorney fully understand your case before deciding how to proceed.

Also, don't assume that you aren't qualified for a Chapter 7 bankruptcy because you make "too much." We try hard to help people qualify for a Chapter 7 bankruptcy if that is their goal (and we agree that it would be best for them). Even if you don't initially qualify, we can use tools such as timing your petition just right or properly performing Means Test calculations to help you obtain your Chapter 7 discharge.

Secured Versus Unsecured Debt

Basically speaking, assets are "secured" if they were used as collateral for a loan. For most people, their secured assets are their car and house. If you want to buy a house, you go to a bank, borrow money, and agree to a mortgage. In essence, you pledged the house as security for the loan. If you don't pay back the loan, the bank takes the house. Your loan to the bank is a secured debt. This is called a "purchase money security interest."

You can also use your assets to secure loans for other reasons. A home equity loan is a great example. Let's say your house is worth $100,000 and your mortgage principal balance is $80,000. You have $20,000 in equity in your home. If you want to put in a new kitchen and need a loan to pay for it you could go to the bank and offer your equity as collateral for a second mortgage or home equity line of credit on the house. This bank now also has a security interest in your home (but it would be "junior" to the original bank).

Another example of a secured loan is a car title loan. Assume you own your car outright...you either bought it in cash or paid off the car note. Now, you need a small loan to pay for repairs, bills, or vacations and you go to a loan company. When you offer your car as collateral the loan company will be a secured creditor. If you don't pay back the loan, the lender will take the car.

Unsecured loans are typically things like credit cards and medical bills. When you go to the doctor you don't offer him your car in exchange for medical services. And, for most folks, when you sign up for a credit card you just agree to pay for your purchases. Most credit cards don't require you to give them something as collateral.

Please don't get a title loan for a vacation or any other purpose that is not absolutely necessary. The interest rates are just too high and the terms are stiff.
It's not worth it!

Why the fuss?

Secured creditors get priority when you can't pay everyone. There are different types of security interests and there are lots of steps involved for the creditor to make sure they have a "perfected" security interest, but if they do their job right they will get paid before you pay other creditors in bankruptcy. They can also use their security interest to take back the property to satisfy the debt. That's why your house can be foreclosed upon and your car repossessed. You promised in advance to give the creditor that asset if you didn't pay your bills.

But, here's the kicker. Even if the creditor takes back the asset when you don't pay your bills, if you owe more than the asset is worth, the creditor can still sue you for the difference. For example, if you owe $5,000 on your car, but it's only worth $3,000, the loan company can repossess the car and still sue you for $2,000! The same is true for your house. In this market, if you are "underwater" and the bank forecloses you could lose your house and still have to pay tens of thousands of dollars to make up the difference in a "short sale."

The Truth About Student Loans

Years ago, certain student loans were dischargeable in bankruptcy. In 2005 Congress changed the bankruptcy laws and said that no student loans could be discharged, no matter whether they were federal or private loans.

So, what happened next? There was a huge explosion in the amount of private loans. Private student loan lenders were no longer worried about having their loans discharged in a bankruptcy, so they offered them to anyone and everyone.

Then, because loans were so easy to get, schools kept raising their tuition costs and new schools popped up overnight offering education programs that weren't worth a tenth of what was charged for them.

Recently, graduates have sued some of these schools alleging the school overpromised students about what jobs they could get, whether they could pass licensing exams, or whether the school's program would actually give them the skills they needed for the job.

Employers have said that the students hired from some of these schools are less prepared than a high school student. Somehow these schools, despite charging tens of thousands of dollars in tuition, actually decreased their students' job-readiness. But, banks don't care about that. The money was borrowed and it has to be repaid.

We have spent many hours talking to Congress attempting to persuade them to reconsider the stance on student loans.

Our clients are in great distress trying to pay huge loans while being unable to secure a job that pays them what they're worth. It's time for Congress to recognize the impact of their decision to prevent the discharge of student loans in bankruptcy. But, until that happens there are some things we can do to help.

Even though student loans cannot be discharged through typical bankruptcy filings right now, there are still some options available.

- Consolidate loans to reduce your interest rate
- Negotiate with your lenders to reduce your rate or payment amount
- Structure payments based on current income
- Reduce or eliminate other debt to make it easier to pay your student loans

Under some circumstances, it's possible to wipe out debt for tuition and fees in a bankruptcy. This is money owed directly to the school, not to a student loan lender.

THE BRUNNER TEST – HOPE FOR SOME

The rule is that student loans are not dischargeable in bankruptcy, but there are exceptions to every rule. If you can pass the Brunner Test, you may be able to discharge your loans. But, this test has been described as "draconian" because it seems to require absolute poverty with no chance of recovery in order to have student loans forgiven. It's not quite that harsh, but it is pretty close.

How Many Times Can I File?

During the reign of Genghis Khan in East Asia, you would be sentenced to death if you went bankrupt three times. Thankfully, there's no such rule in the United States. Sometimes things happen in life that put you in the position to need to file for bankruptcy again. Don't worry…it happens to a lot of people. The Bankruptcy Code allows for subsequent filings so that you to discharge your debts every few years if necessary.

You can file bankruptcy as many times as you need to, but there are waiting periods that you must know before you file.

Successive Chapter 7s - 8 Years

If you file a Chapter 7 bankruptcy and receive a discharge, you cannot receive a second Chapter 7 discharge in any Chapter 7 case that is filed within 8 years.

Successive Chapter 13s – 2 Years

If you file a Chapter 13 and receive a discharge, you cannot receive a second Chapter 13 discharge in any Chapter 13 case that is filed within 2 years.

Chapter 13, Then Chapter 7 – 6 Years

If you file a Chapter 13 and receive a discharge, you cannot receive a discharge under any Chapter 7 case that is filed within 6 years. However, there are a few exceptions that could help you file faster if needed.

Chapter 7, Then Chapter 13 – 4 Years

If you file a Chapter 7 and receive a discharge, you cannot receive a Chapter 13 discharge in any Chapter 13 case that is filed within 4 years.

It's the Discharge that Matters

The waiting periods described apply to *discharges*, not to *filing*. A discharge means that your case was effectively completed and the dischargeable debts in your case were discharged (i.e., wiped out or forgiven).

If you file a case and it is *dismissed*, you can usually file again right away. However, there may be a 180-day waiting period if your case was dismissed for certain reasons. Before filing again and spending the filing fee, check with an experienced bankruptcy attorney to make sure this waiting period does not apply to your case.

> If your second case is a Chapter 13 and for some reason the plan is not confirmed you may not have the option to convert to a Chapter 7 like other debtors. You would have to make sure that the filing of the second case would have to conform to the waiting periods above, which are longer for Chapter 7s.

What if Your Discharge Was Denied?

If your discharge was denied in your first case, you may be able to file again, but you will probably not be entitled to a discharge of the debts included in your first case. Things get tricky here and you would benefit from the advice of an experienced bankruptcy lawyer.

Save What Matters to You While Eliminating Debt

Save Your Reputation: Bankruptcy is Not a Dirty Word

Many people look at bankruptcy as a failure or something only for people who can't manage their money or spend too much. But, in the U.S. 90% of bankruptcies are filed because of job loss, medical bills, or divorce. Trust us, job loss can happen to anyone. And, we all know the statistic that 50% of marriages end in divorce. As for medical bills, one accident, illness, or even a pregnancy can put any of us in the poor house these days.

There is no way that you can predict these types of events. No one gets married believing they will be divorced. And, no one drives off in the morning believing they will be in a car accident. But, it can happen to any of us, at any time.

> *Believe it or not, I was hit by a snowplow while walking to the store as a teenager and couldn't work or go to school for weeks. It can happen to anyone!*
> *~Kelly*

Yes, some people find themselves needing to file bankruptcy because of poor choices, but in our practice, that's the exception rather than the rule. And, when poor choices are to blame, they often happened a long time ago. According to the lender Sallie Mae, 60%

of college seniors have credit cards. And, at least one financial magazine reports that college students put 15% of their monthly expenses on credit cards. These students are typically piling on debt while they're not earning much (or anything). By the time they graduate college, these students have an overload of credit card and student loan debt – even before they have their first "real job".

Bankruptcy is a tool. It is available to all of us whenever we need it. It is not a welfare program or bailout. It is a recognition that our economy and our society as a whole is better off when families are financially stable. To get there we sometimes need to forgive some debts and let people start over. While that may temporarily hurt the bottom line of the creditor (is anyone crying for the bank?), in the long run it is better for everyone to get a family back on their feet.

Bankruptcy has been around since the time of the Old Testament. Whether you believe in Christianity or not, in the Old Testament, every seventh year is decreed as a Sabbatical Year when the release of all debts owed by members of the community is mandated. The seventh Sabbatical Year (every 49 years) is the Year of Jubilee when all debts are released for community members and foreigners alike, and all "debt-slaves" are released.

Bankruptcy, or at least a means to relieve your debts in a manner other than payment, existed in almost every civilized society. Ancient Greeks allowed for indentured servitude to pay off debts and were given protection from harm during that time. In East Asia, documents show that bankruptcy was allowed under the reign of Genghis Khan. In 1542, the Statute of Bankrupts was written into English law to allow for the orderly discharge of debts.

Bankruptcy is nothing new. People have been in your position for centuries. Just be thankful that we have a modern system that makes it relatively quick, easy, and painless to file for bankruptcy – without the need for indentured servitude!

Save Your Credit: How Bankruptcy Can Actually Improve Your Credit

Believe it or not, most people have better credit scores after filing for bankruptcy than they did before.

Think about it this way.... Your credit score is like a house built brick by brick by each of your financial activities. When you have late payments, penalties, and fees, those bricks start crumbling and the house falls down. It's hard to rebuild with all that rubble in the way.

Recently, a client told us that immediately after filing for bankruptcy her credit score INCREASED by nearly 70 points! For her, this was likely because all of her debt was in collections. Now that she filed for bankruptcy, a high amount of debt was going away and no new negative marks were going to be added in relation to her soon-to-be discharged debt.
--Kelly

What bankruptcy does is to wipe the foundation clean so that you can rebuild on stable ground. Even if your credit score declines when you file for bankruptcy, as most do, our clients often find that after a few years their credit scores are higher than they were before they filed. In fact, you'll probably start getting new credit card offers as soon as your bankruptcy is final.

Think about it this way ... If you were a lender, would you rather lend to someone who had a bunch of debt and was falling behind on payments or a person who had a previous bankruptcy, but no current debt? In that way, bankruptcy filers may actually be attractive to lenders.

There are steps you can take to rebuild your credit once you have a clean slate. For example:

- Accept, and use, a small credit card. Preferably a secured card – one where you pay a deposit to the credit card company as security for the credit line they extend.
- Continue to pay the secured loans that you kept through your bankruptcy – like your house and car.
- Review your credit report a few months after your bankruptcy to make sure all creditors are reporting correctly.
- Get utilities in your name (gas, electric, cell phone) and pay them on time and in full each month.

> Don't let your creditors keep reporting bad information on your report. If a creditor violates the Fair Credit Reporting Act or your bankruptcy discharge, you can sue them for damages and they will have to pay your attorneys' fees.

We offer a free credit report review for all of our completed bankruptcy clients.

We also recommend enrolling in a credit monitoring service within three years of your bankruptcy discharge. This will help you monitor what is happening with your credit. We have found that people who pay attention to their credit score actually make better financial decisions in the future.

Save Your Options: I lost my job, should I file for bankruptcy now?

Most lawyers would welcome you in and happily take your payment to file for bankruptcy. But, our question is: *will you be able to take advantage of your fresh start if you file now?*

Job loss happens to nearly everyone. And for most of us without a financial safety net, a job loss results in the immediate buildup of debt. In this economy it's taking people longer to find jobs and some never find a job that pays as well as the one they lost. Every month they go unemployed or underemployed, the debt rises.

So, let's file for bankruptcy and wipe out all of that debt! Sounds good, right? But…

Let's say we wipe out all your credit card debt, medical bills, back taxes, past due rent, and overdue utilities, what happens next month? If you're still not working, the debt is just going to come back and pile up again each month.

For many people, filing bankruptcy while they are still unemployed is not the best idea. We have counseled many families and advised them to wait. And, there are things we can do in the meantime to negotiate debts down, stop harassing phone calls, and shift the money you do have to the right people.

Also, if a Chapter 13 bankruptcy (repayment plan) is your best option because you have assets to save, your plan is not going to be approved if you have no way of making the proposed plan payments.

Remember, after filing bankruptcy, you must wait anywhere from 4 to 8 years before you can file again (depending on which Chapter you file under). If you file at the beginning of your financial distress you might not get the full benefit of bankruptcy protection.

Every case is different and every families' needs are different. Be sure that you investigate the benefits, costs, and risks to filing bankruptcy and determine, strategically, when the best time to file is for you and your family.

Save Your Marriage: Bankruptcy and Divorce

Financial difficulty is one of the leading reasons why people decide to divorce. But, the divorce may not solve your financial problems. Planning ahead can help you protect more assets, discharge more debt, and either bring you closer to your spouse or allow you to truly separate financially from your spouse.

It's hard to connect to the people you once were when you're laboring under a mountain of debt. Blame is something we see much too often, but often times it's misplaced. Medical bills, job loss, or injury are quite often the true culprits behind the financial collapse of a marriage.

Bankruptcy isn't a cure to all marital woes, but it can certainly clear away some of the obstacles to thinking rationally on an emotional subject. Even when the marriage does subsequently fail, bankruptcy can help both parties find themselves better able to be financially independent without the burden of marital and personal debt weighing them down.

Just remember, the timing is critical. For some people, filing a joint bankruptcy before divorce can be advantageous. For others, there are more options available when filing after the divorce is final. There are some extra protections for joint assets (like your house) that are available only while you're still married. But, waiting to file until the divorce is final can help you qualify for a Chapter 7 or reach other independent financial goals, such as refinancing a house.

If you're considering a divorce and are under financial stress, take a moment to meet with a skilled bankruptcy attorney to consider how bankruptcy can help you make a clean break from your spouse.

A bankruptcy attorney trained in Collaborative Law can be particularly helpful in providing advice to both spouses in an amicable divorce. You or your divorce attorney can contact a Collaborative Bankruptcy Attorney to join in on the divorce process and help everyone come out ahead.

Save Your Retirement Account: Protecting Exempt Assets

Most people will do anything to avoid filing for bankruptcy. They will sell their assets, pawn their wedding rings, and use all of their savings – including retirement accounts to pay their creditors. But, that is a bad idea.

We get it. We know people want to do "the right thing" and to pay back debts they incurred. But, it breaks our heart when people pay off dischargeable debts with exempt assets. Why? Because exempt assets are protected from your creditors in a bankruptcy for a reason. For example, there is a public benefit to you having funds to draw on in retirement instead of relying solely on social security because those who only have social security generally need additional public assistance. The same is true for home equity. People often use their home equity to fund their retirement. Isn't that the American Dream? Some states offer greater protection to home equity than others, but every home owner can take advantage of this "homestead exemption" to protect at least some of their equity. And, married couples can usually protect even greater equity than unmarried home owners.

These exemptions allow you to file for bankruptcy, eliminate your debt, and still walk away with your life insurance, retirement accounts, and home equity. This will help you to truly take advantage of your fresh start.

Examples of Exempt Property:

- ERISA-qualified retirement plans (e.g., 401(k) Plans)
- Life insurance
- State employee pensions
- Home equity up to a certain amount (more if you and your spouse own the house together)

There is strategy involved in "exemption planning" to help maximize your protections under the Bankruptcy Code. An attorney with experience in bankruptcy can help you keep as much of your property as possible under the law. In fact, in our practice, most people who file a Chapter 7 bankruptcy are considered "no asset filers" and they are not required to sell any property in order to relieve themselves of their debt. Your case may be different, but proper planning can lead to be best possible outcome.

Don't use an exempt asset to pay a dischargeable debt without seeking the advice of a lawyer.

As a general rule, you should never cash in an exempt asset (like your 401(k) retirement plan) to pay for something we could help you discharge in bankruptcy (like your credit card debt). When people wait to talk to a lawyer they often make choices they regret later. We've seen many families sell all their property, and cash in exempt assets like life insurance policies and their children's savings accounts to pay their credit card bills. This not only makes us sad, but it also increases the likelihood that the family will be in financial trouble again later. Please don't make that mistake.

Save Your Health: Medical Bills and Bankruptcy

It's an oft-repeated truth that Medical issues are a leading cause of bankruptcies. Even when an injury or illness doesn't cause long term unemployment or disability, the simple cost of treatment can overwhelm even the most financially stable people.

Many of us now have "high deductible plans" where we are required to pay the first $5,000 or $10,000 (or more!) of our health care out of pocket before insurance steps in. Then, after the insurance starts to cover treatment, we still have to pay copays that average 20% of certain procedures. 20% of an emergency surgery or pregnancy complication, for example, can create overwhelming debt for anyone. And, that's what happens if you have "good" insurance.

Did you know?
Someone who is uninsured is charged many times more for the same medical procedures as people who have even a high deductible insurance policy?

This is because they lack negotiating power. Insurance companies negotiate lower payments on all services for doctors who want to be "in network" and have access to that group of patients. Even people who pay out of pocket for health care due to "high deductible plans" get the benefit of the reduced costs. Yet, people without insurance pay the maximum rate. A simple blood test that might cost $3 for an insured person, could be $750 for someone without insurance. And, don't even get us started on hospital stays or surgery costs! Then to make matters worse, that uninsured person is now also forced to pay a separate penalty to the Federal Government in addition to the premium prices they are charged by doctors.

If you get sick, are injured, or otherwise couldn't work for a period of time, how long would it be until your savings is depleted, your credit maxed out, and you're on the verge of financial ruin? All too often people find that this number is less than 3 months. As a society, we carry an enormous amount of debt when times are good, so when disaster strikes, we only have savings to fall back on and there frequently isn't nearly enough of that to keep us afloat.

We recommend that our clients maintain at least 3 months of income in savings to help them through temporary emergencies without having to fall back on credit cards. That's something that is often impossible to accomplish before bankruptcy.

Save Your Cash: Maximizing Exemptions

Your "Bankruptcy Estate" is considered a snapshot in time. It is frozen at the time you file for bankruptcy protection. So, if you file when you have $10,000 in assets that's what you have. Even if the next day you have $12,000 in assets, in most cases, your Bankruptcy Estate will still only be worth $10,000.

Exemptions are what allow you to protect your property. Knowing what can and cannot be protected and knowing what doesn't need that protection is one of the toughest things to do with your case. Poor planning and less than optimal exemption use have cost bankruptcy filers millions in unnecessary property seizures – especially those that file without the help of an experienced bankruptcy attorney.

How complex is it? Well, did you know that if you make a payment to a creditor before filing, that payment can be seized so that it can be spread out to your other creditors? You probably don't care if it's Visa or MasterCard whose money is seized, but what if that creditor having money seized is your Mom?

Also, some assets can be entirely exempt if they're kept separate from other assets, but when mixed, you will be forced to use up valuable personal exemptions to protect them. For example, keeping separate bank accounts for different types of income (Social Security, Pension, your spouse's W2 earnings), can help you keep cash out of your Bankruptcy Estate, which means you get to keep it even while you discharge your debts! Knowing these rules is as important to your family as it is to you.

If you are considering filing for bankruptcy, some pre-filing exemption planning can help you keep more of your property. Most states will allow you to engage in some form of exemption planning, but as we've discussed already, any attempt to defraud your creditors by hiding assets or giving preference to certain creditors will not be permitted.

Timing your filing strategically can also help you maximize your exemptions. If you have lived in this state for less than 2 years, we may be able to use the exemptions of your previous state, which could be more favorable. We may also be able to take advantage of Federal exemptions.

Another example of timing strategy is when your income is inconsistent. If you receive a large bonus or commission or earn less in the summer than during the school year, you may want to time your filing when your income is lowest. This may allow you to qualify more easily for a Chapter 7. Also, if you are about to receive that large bonus or tax refund, it may be best to wait until you've spent some of that money (on basic living expenses, not luxury purchases!) before filing so that you do not need to worry about finding exemption room for that money.

We may also advise you to spend some nonexempt assets by prepaying some basic living expenses, such as paying your rent a little early or prepaying your next auto insurance bill. This helps you to reduce your bank account (a generally nonexempt asset) while saving your post-petition income (a non-Bankruptcy Estate asset). But, again, be careful here. If your exemption planning is excessive, it may be viewed as a fraud on your creditors.

Exemption planning and bankruptcy strategy is where a skilled bankruptcy attorney becomes invaluable. If you go to an attorney who does not file many bankruptcies or if you try to file your case on your own you may end up losing money instead of getting the fresh start you need.

Save Yourself from Fines and Penalties: Beware the Bankruptcy Abuse Prevention and Consumer Protection Act

On April 20, 2005, the Bankruptcy Abuse Prevention and Consumer Protection Act (BAPCPA) came into effect and dramatically changed bankruptcy law, including who could file for bankruptcy and when. The new law creates many traps for filers (and attorneys) in an effort to keep people from "abusing" the bankruptcy system. One of the biggest traps is the new "Means Test" requirement to qualify for a Chapter 7.

How to pass the Means Test:

The Easy Way

If your income is lower than the median income of all households in your state with the same number of people, you qualify for a Chapter 7 bankruptcy without any more work.

The Somewhat Easy Way

There are three exceptions to the Means Test that allow certain people to bypass the test even if their income is higher than the median income for similar households in their state. If you have a lot of business debt, are a disabled veteran, or were recently on active duty from the military reserves of National Guard, you may qualify.

The Hard Way

If your income is above the state median and you don't qualify for one of the exemptions above, you must pass through the Means Test to qualify for a Chapter 7. Walking through the Means Test is a lot like filling out IRS tax forms. There are a lot of questions about your income and expenses to calculate your monthly "disposable income". The starting point is your average monthly income over the six months immediately before filing for bankruptcy. This means there's some strategy involved in deciding when to file if your income isn't consistent because of bonuses, commissions, summer pay, etc.

Next, you deduct your monthly expenses from that income. The IRS prescribes certain default values for common expenses, and you can use those values or your actual, documented expenses. Perhaps you take prescription medication that costs $300 per month even after insurance. Or, maybe you have an outrageous monthly condominium fee for your residence. When properly calculated, you can include these exceptional expenses in the Means Test to help you qualify for a Chapter 7.

There is an art to the Means Test that can only be mastered with experience. If you hope to file a Chapter 7 bankruptcy and you’re over the median income, be sure to contact an experienced bankruptcy attorney for assistance.

And, Sometimes You Don’t Pass…And That’s OK Too

Chapter 13 bankruptcies are still a valuable tool and a good option for many families. Even though a Chapter 13 is considered a “repayment plan” you may still be able to complete your plan without paying off all of your debts. For example, your unsecured creditors (*e.g.*, credit cards, medical bills) may be paid little or nothing under your Chapter 13 plan.

The Means Test involves a long list of possible expenses. Some online calculators suggest that you can analyze your Means Test qualifications yourself simply by typing in a few numbers, but it is far more complex. For each requested expense there is a standard amount predetermined for people filing in your region. But, a skilled attorney can often use your actual expenses to override this standard.

We once had a flight attendant as a client. She was required for her job to maintain a certain standard of appearance. We were able to justify claiming her exceptional makeup and grooming expenses to qualify her and her husband for a Chapter 7 bankruptcy even though they had a six figure income!

--Will

Remember, even if you pass the Means Test, Chapter 7 might not be right for you.

Sometimes a Chapter 13 bankruptcy is still the better solution for people who otherwise qualify for a Chapter 7. A Chapter 13, for example, allows you to cure a default on your mortgage and keep your house. Also, if you "voluntarily" enter a Chapter 13 even though you qualified for a Chapter 7 you may be able to enter into a shorter repayment plan.

Save Your Car: Chapter 7 Redemption Loans

You might have heard that you can reduce the amount you owe on a car to the car's actual value. But, most people, including many lawyers, think this option is only available to Chapter 13 filers. Not true! Chapter 7 filers can take advantage of this option too, but in a different way.

Our clients have been successful at using "Redemption Loans" to take advantage of an often overlooked tool in the Bankruptcy Code. Section 722 of the Bankruptcy Code allows Chapter 7 filers to "redeem" cars and other secured household property. This means that you can essentially offer to buy the property from the lien holder for the amount it's actually worth.

In short, what you do is to obtain a loan through a special redemption loan provider that gives you the cash you need to buy the car for its current value. The remaining balance then becomes an unsecured debt that is discharged along with your debt.

Caution! Redemption Loans can be a great tool, but they are not always a good idea. Some of the things we need to consider include: whether there is a co-debtor on the loan, what the interest rate is on the loan, how much is owed, and the condition of the car.

Example

You still owe Ford Motor Credit $15,000 for your car, but it's only worth $10,000. You can obtain a "redemption loan" for $10,000 from a company specializing in these types of loans. You then offer Ford Motor Credit the $10,000 in exchange for a clear title. The Bankruptcy Code requires that they accept this offer if it represents the fair market value of the car. Ford Motor Credit cannot come after you for the balance (but, if there is any money to be distributed in your bankruptcy, they can stand in line with all other unsecured creditors, like Visa and Mastercard).

As you'll learn later in this book, we can use "Cramdowns" in a Chapter 13 bankruptcy to reduce the amount you owe on a car to the actual value of the car.

Save Your Time: Complete Your Bankruptcy in as Little as 90 Days

Simple Chapter 7 bankruptcies can often be completed in around 90 days from filing. As soon as you meet with us we begin drafting your Petition for Bankruptcy. We can file a complete Chapter 7 Petition in just a few days if needed. From then, there is one quick meeting at the Court – called a Meeting of the Creditors – and then your case is closed.

Filing your bankruptcy today can mean immediately stopping a garnishment or a foreclosure!

Most clients we see for Chapter 7 cases are considered "no asset filers" because we are able to protect all of their assets with applicable exemptions. So, there is nothing for the Bankruptcy Trustee to seize or sell to pay your debts. This means that your case can be over with one simple meeting with the Trustee at the Meeting of Creditors. And, by the way, in 99% of our Chapter 7 cases no actual creditors show up at that meeting so don't fear!

A skilled attorney can help you qualify for a Chapter 7 bankruptcy even if others think you may be required to file a Chapter 13 bankruptcy, which could take up to 5 years to complete. The key to qualifying for a Chapter 7 bankruptcy is to pass the Means Test. The Means Test is based on your household income and expenses. It is quite an art for an attorney to use a combination of both actual expenses and the estimated expenses allowed by law to maximize your chances of qualifying for a Chapter 7.

Save Your Paycheck: Stop Wage Garnishments Today

Many of our clients ignore or avoid their financial problems. They just stop opening their mail, stop answering their phone, and essentially bury their head in the sand hoping it will all go away. Before they know what is happening, they have a judgment entered against them, a lien on their wages and suddenly 25% of their income is garnished. Most people we know would be in big trouble if they suddenly lost 25% of their pay.

Creditors with a judgment against you for a debt can easily garnish your wages just by sending the proper paperwork to your employer. The employer is then required to give your creditor 25% of your after-tax pay. And, other creditors can line up to garnish you as soon as the first one is done.

Filing for bankruptcy will stop wage garnishments and even tax levies immediately.

Once a bankruptcy petition is filed, all garnishments must stop. A creditor with a judgment does not have priority over another. So, by collecting money through a garnishment, that creditor is getting an impermissible "preference" payment. All collection actions and legal proceedings that might affect your assets must stop immediately once you have filed for bankruptcy.

We can file a bankruptcy petition in one day if we need to. As soon as the petition is filed, we send a notice of filing to your employer and the creditor to stop the garnishment. In many cases, we can even get them to return some or all of the garnished money to you!

We can also stop a garnishment if your income is too low to allow for a legal garnishment. This is the first time making too little will actually be a good thing!

Don't let your creditor take your hard earned money right from your paycheck. And, stop struggling to make ends meet with a garnished paycheck. Let us help!

Save Your House: Stop Foreclosure

Did you know that simply by filing a bankruptcy petition, a foreclosure sale MUST STOP IMMEDIATELY? We have literally sent notices of bankruptcy to auction houses just minutes before a sale was to take place in order to save our clients' houses.

While it's true that not everyone can (or should) save their house in a bankruptcy, filing a petition for bankruptcy will immediately stop the foreclosure proceedings and give you time to figure out what is best for your family.

Just stopping a foreclosure may not be enough. You need a plan of action to get caught back up on your mortgage payments if you want to stay in your home. There are several strategies to consider:

- Mortgage modification. There are numerous Federal and lender-based programs available to help you reduce your monthly payment and restructure your loan to make it work with your current income.
- Principal reduction. Several programs offer the ability to reduce the amount you owe if you owe more than your house is worth. This will reduce your monthly payments and/or the length of your loan.
- Bankruptcy. Through bankruptcy, you can either wipe out your back debt (and any loss you took on the sale or foreclosure of the house) or create a structured payment plan

to help you pay the back mortgage payments off over 3 to 5 years without the interest!

> Did you know that in some cases your Homeowners' Association can foreclose on your home if you are behind on payments? If you've gotten behind, call us and we will help.

I came home from the beach one day to find a FORECLOSURE notice on my front door and my house was set to be sold in 2 weeks! It turns out that the company servicing my mortgage changed (and didn't tell me) and they did not forward my payments. After a lot of sleepless nights and mountains of paperwork, it finally got resolved and I kept my house. Although this was just a mistake for me, it's a reality for a lot of our clients. If you ever get a foreclosure notice, don't wait! Call us and we will help you save your house too.

--Kelly

We can stop foreclosure proceedings with as little as one day's notice in some cases. Even if you think you're out of time to save your house, call us. Don't give up!

Save Your Tax Refund: Discharge Old Tax Debt

If you're like most Americans, you look forward to your tax refund every year and have probably already thought about how you were going to spend it. A vacation? New furniture? Paying bills?

But, if you owe old taxes from prior years, you won't see your refund. If you are due a refund, the IRS (or State Tax Authority) will just take the refund and apply it to the old tax debt. Other creditors can intercept your refund too. For example, if you owe back payments on federal student loans, child support, Social Security, Small Business Association Loans, or just about any federal loan program, they can take your refund before you even see it!

Don't be discouraged. We can save your refund.

Certain tax debts can be discharged (wiped out) in bankruptcy. There are some tricky rules that are based on when/if you filed your tax return and when the tax was assessed, but if they are eligible we can have the entire balance forgiven.

> **Timing matters**. If you file for bankruptcy too soon, you may not be eligible to discharge your tax debt. Consult with an experienced bankruptcy attorney before filing if you have old tax debt.

The IRS and State Tax Authorities are not immune from bankruptcy protection. The bankruptcy laws allow you wipe out tax debt – take advantage of it. Don't struggle any longer to pay old tax debt.

We had one client with over $1 MILLION in back tax debt. After just one meeting with our attorneys we had a plan to get rid of all of that debt with no payment to the IRS. *And, in just a few months, our client got a discharge through a Chapter 7 bankruptcy. They were not required to pay anything to the IRS for this old debt, and they got to keep their house, their car, their retirement savings, and more. This client suffered and sacrificed for years trying to pay off this enormous debt and we wiped it out in a matter of months.*

--Will

Save Your Phone Minutes: Let Us Talk to Your Creditors

If you are behind on payments, you know that your creditors will call you day and night to hound you for money. They will call your home, cell, or office, they may even come to your house to try to collect.

Although the Fair Debt Collection Act places restrictions on when, where, and how they contact you, collection agencies are notoriously bad at following those rules.

Our clients have heard some ridiculous things from collection agencies, such as:

- You can't discharge this debt in bankruptcy. Your contract says so.
- You will go to jail if you don't pay.
- You will lose your job if you don't pay.
- Your [mother, father, sister, brother, spouse, best friend] will have to pay if you don't even though they didn't open the account with you.
- We're sending the Sherriff to come get you right now.

These are all false.

Our firm offers a Creditors Line where you can direct all of your creditors to call.

As soon as you've hired us to file for bankruptcy or negotiate your debt, tell all of your creditors to contact us directly. We know how to handle them.

And, if they ever contact you again after you've told them that we are your attorneys, we may be able to sue them for violating the Fair Debt Collection Act. We love to catch creditors in violations, especially "junk debt" buyers who buy very old debt. Not only do you get money when they do something wrong, but we get our fees paid too!

Don't waste another minute talking to your creditors (or avoiding your phone when it rings). Turn them over to us.

Save Your Job: Don't Let Your Debt Impact Your Work

For most people, filing for bankruptcy has no impact on your current job. Federal law states that no private employer can terminate employment or discriminate against someone who has filed for bankruptcy (or is related to someone who filed).

What will impact your job, however, is debt. If your phone is ringing off the hook from creditors or they are calling or visiting your job, this can look bad for you. Also, the stress of dealing with overwhelming debt can impact your performance. Then, if you are hit with a garnishment, your employer will be required to pay some of your wages to your creditor on your behalf.

Most employers these days run a credit check on all potential new hires. Although your bankruptcy may show up depending on the search they run, your discharged debt will not show as a current liability. Our research shows that most employers would rather hire a person with a bankruptcy, no debt, and evidence that they are rebuilding their credit, than a person suffering under the weight of large debt.

What about security clearances? Credit counselors for the military, CIA, and FBI, have explained that a person with financial problems is at high risk for blackmail. Filing for bankruptcy and eliminating your debt helps you lower that risk, thus making you a better candidate for the security clearance than you once were.

And, remember, the courts no longer publish a list of bankruptcy filers in the local paper as a matter of course. For your boss to find out that you've filed for bankruptcy, you would either have to tell him or he would have to take the time to search the public records for your name. Most employers do not have the time to do those searches and most are not worried about people who take charge of their debt and use the bankruptcy system as it was intended.

The Fair Debt Collection Act allows you to tell most creditors that they can no longer contact you at work, but this usually happens after they have already tried at least once.

Special Chapter 13 Tools

Save Your House: Using Lien Stripping

Lien stripping is a tool available in Chapter 13 bankruptcies that allow you to eliminate a "wholly unsecured" lien on your property. This happens most often with houses and cars. When more than one loan is secured by the same property, there is an order of priority specified by law. Usually, the first lien filed or the lien used to purchase the property has the number 1 position and all other liens are "junior" in the order they were recorded on the property's title. If the property is foreclosed on and sold, the lenders will be paid in the order of priority. That's why a second mortgage usually has a higher interest rate – they run the risk of not getting paid if the house is foreclosed upon and sold for less than the total due to both the first and second mortgages.

Example:

You buy a house worth $100,000. Bank A approves you for a loan for $80,000 and you plan to put down $10,000. So, you go to Bank B and ask for a second loan to pay for the remaining $10,000. Now there are 2 loans on the property, a first mortgage of $80,000 and a second mortgage of $10,000.

Now, you're considering bankruptcy and your house is worth less than you paid for it. An appraisal shows the house is worth $75,000. If the house was foreclosed upon and sold for $75,000, the first mortgage company would get $75,000 of the $80,000 it is owed and the second mortgage company would get nothing. The second loan is now considered "wholly unsecured" because the value of the house cannot secure both houses.

A Chapter 13 bankruptcy can "strip" the junior, second lien from the property if you file a motion with the proper paperwork and documentation.

What happens to the stripped lien?

Once stripped, the lender must remove the lien from your property. The stripped lien then gets the same treatment as other unsecured debts, such as your credit cards. In a Chapter 13, general unsecured debts often receive little or no payment and are discharged at the completion of your Chapter 13 plan without any penalty.

Save Your House: Repaying Debt Slowly With No More Interest or Late Penalties

A Chapter 13 bankruptcy allows you up to 5 years to repay certain debts while eliminating others. If you are far behind on house payments, but you want to keep your house, you can use your time in a Chapter 13 bankruptcy to repay the back house debts while still eliminating all or most of your other debts.

Debts in a Chapter 13 bankruptcy are classified as secured, priority unsecured, or general unsecured and are treated differently. Your mortgage debt is secured by your house. Unsecured debt for most people is things like credit cards and medical bills. Priority unsecured debt includes tax debt, back child support, and other overdue domestic support obligations.

You can structure a Chapter 13 plan to pay back your secured debt, like your house, while discharging some or all of your general unsecured debt. As long as you keep making your plan payments, you'll walk away with your house without having to pay everyone else. And, during your Chapter 13 plan, no interest or penalties will be added to the back mortgage debt!

When you file a Chapter 13 bankruptcy, you propose a repayment plan to the Bankruptcy Trustee. That plan must be affordable for you even if it means that your general unsecured creditors receive little or no payment. The payment for the general unsecured creditors is based on a percentage of what is owed based on your disposable income and the value of your bankruptcy estate. In short, the general unsecured creditors must receive at least what they would have gotten if you had filed a Chapter 7 bankruptcy (which, for many filers is $0!).

Now you have time to make up your back house payments, while still getting to discharge most, if not all, of your other unsecured debt just as you would have in a Chapter 7. It's the best of both worlds for some filers.

Save Your Car: Using Cramdowns to Reduce Your Car Loan

Another benefit that Chapter 13s have over Chapter 7 bankruptcies is the ability to reduce the balance owed on certain secured debts in process known as a cramdown. With a cramdown you can reduce the principal balance of your loan to the market value of the property. A cramdown is most often used on car loans.

Example:

You own a car worth $4,000, but your outstanding balance on your car note is $7,000. With a Chapter 13 cramdown, we can petition the Court to reduce the amount of secured debt under the car note to $4,000. In other words, the first $4,000 of the $7,000 owed is secured and the rest is unsecured. Then, the remaining $3,000 that is now unsecured becomes part of the pool of other general unsecured creditors and is often discharged entirely or paid very little.

Key Questions:

1. Is the debt secured?
2. Do you owe more than the car is worth?
3. If cramming down a car: Did you purchase the car at least 910 days prior to filing for bankruptcy (approximately 2 ½ years ago)?

If cramming down other property: Did you purchase the property at least one year prior to bankruptcy?

4. Do you have a high interest rate? A Chapter 13 cramdown can reduce your interest rate to a more reasonable market rate.
5. How long do you have left to pay? You generally pay the remaining balance of a crammed down loan over the length of the Plan, so you may be able to stretch out your payments up to another 5 years.

> A cramdown is not available to reduce the balance on the mortgage on your home, but it may be available for investment property if you can pay the reduced mortgage within the plan.

Save Your Interest Payments: Build Your Own Wealth, Not Your Creditors

Do you know someone without a credit card? We don't. Nowadays you can't check out at your local Target or Walmart without being asked three times if you want one of their credit cards. And, then there's all of the offers on the mail. For people in financial trouble, it's easy to see why getting more credit cards seems like a good idea. No one expects their financial troubles to last a long time. It makes sense to get one more card to help you through the rough time. Everyone expects to be able to pay off their credit cards with their next job, next raise, next tax refund… but, that doesn't always happen and it just snowballs.

Did you know that when you pay the minimum payment on your credit card you are still accruing interest? At over 18% interest for the average credit card (and up to 75% for some cards!), your balance will keep going up even if you stop using the card and pay the bill every month. Every credit card bill includes a disclosure statement that shows how long it will take you to pay off the card by making the minimum payment. Take a look at one of yours – does it say that it will take you 25 or 30 years? That's typical for a $10,000 to $15,000 credit card balance. That disclosure chart will also tell you that over those 25 or 30 years you'll end up paying more than twice the original debt. Wow.

Think about it this way –
if you only plan to make the minimum payment,
every time you swipe your credit card
you are agreeing to pay
double the amount.

So, that $40 dinner just cost you $80. And, that $100 pair of shoes that you thought were a good deal, aren't that much of a bargain at $200.

But, what if you could stop the interest from building? Instead of paying your cards each month, what if we told you to put those payments toward your own expenses or your savings? Things would be a lot easier, right?

Often our clients say they cannot file for bankruptcy because they cannot afford the filing fees or attorney cost. But, then we tell them to stop paying their credit cards and all of a sudden they have money available. We may give you this advice even if you are not late on your credit cards. You may be uncomfortable with the idea of ignoring a bill, but if you are going to file for bankruptcy there is no need to send your hard earned money to pay a dischargeable debt.

Please don't intentionally stop paying your bills without talking to an attorney first.

We encourage you to prioritize your debt and expenses. If you're filing for bankruptcy, we will show you who to pay and who not to pay and how to wind up with more cash in your pocket.

Let Us Help You!

Save Yourself: Don't Go It Alone

There are many tools available online these days to help people complete legal tasks without a lawyer, even filing for bankruptcy. Can you do it? Yes. Should you do it? No.

We have witnessed so many casualties of self-prepared filings that we could fill a book just with those cautionary tales. The same applies to people who choose a discount lawyer. Not to disparage our profession at all, but in our experience lawyers are like most else – you often get what you pay for.

Common mistakes made by people who file without a lawyer:

1. Picking the wrong Chapter under which to file.
2. Using the wrong forms (or not filing all the necessary forms).
3. Not following all local and Federal rules, including filing fee deadlines, required notice to all creditors, certificates of service, deadlines for submission of documents, refiling dismissed cases without extending the automatic stay.
4. Transferring property to family members before filing thinking they are protecting that property from creditors.
5. Paying off some debts before filing for bankruptcy and creating a "preference" payment.
6. Paying back loans from family members before filing.

7. Improperly using exemptions. If you fail to properly exempt your property, it will be seized by the bankruptcy trustee and sold to pay your creditors.
8. Thinking they failed the Means Test and can't file a Chapter 7.
9. Missing out on opportunities to reduce certain secured debts through lien stripping and cramdowns.
10. Mishandling jointly held property.
11. Taking legal advice from a bankruptcy petition preparer who is unqualified and unauthorized to give that advice or practice law.

Save Your Money: Hire the Grafton Firm

What makes us different from other lawyers?

We offer a FREE CONSULTATION just for reading this book.

Even if you don't plan to hire an attorney, come in, sit down with us, and get some free advice from seasoned attorneys.

We are a family firm.

William and Kelly Grafton started this firm because they wanted to bring "big firm" advice to every family. We take great pride in providing personal service and direct access to our attorneys. We give you our cell phone numbers and do our best to answer your calls at any time. We will personally represent you at your Chapter 7 Meeting of Creditors or Chapter 13 Plan Confirmation.

So many times we go to a Meeting of Creditors and see lawyers walk into the waiting room with a list of names – clients they have never met. At other firms, one lawyer (or even a paralegal) meets with you and discusses your case, another prepares your petition, a different person answers your questions when you call, and yet another person shows up to represent you in court.

We get holiday cards from our clients, we send baby shower gifts, and we get most of our clients as referrals from other happy clients. That's how we know we're doing good work.

We are willing to turn away prospective clients.

Not everyone should file for bankruptcy. And, even those who should might be better off waiting to file. We will only agree to work for you if we think we can actually help.

We are not a "bankruptcy mill".

One of the main reasons our clients are happy is that we don't take a "one size fits all approach." Every client gets our personal attention and the benefit of our years of practice. You are not just another case to us. Your bankruptcy will be handled from the start by William or Kelly.

We charge a flat fee.

Almost every phone call we get from a prospective client starts with: "how much do you charge?" The short answer is, "we don't know yet." Every case is different. We usually charge a flat fee for filing a bankruptcy, but that fee still depends on how complicated your case is. This has nothing to do with how much you make or how much debt you have. We will sit down with you – FOR FREE – and assess your case. We'll give you advice. And, we'll tell you whether or not we think bankruptcy is right for you.

We don't represent creditors.

In our opinion, it is an inherent conflict of interest to represent both creditors and debtors even if there is no conflict in a given case. Although we have occasionally helped a private person or small business collect a debt, it is a rare case and usually has some very special circumstances. You will not see us collecting for Visa or Mastercard.

We don't take every case that walks in the door.

As attorneys licensed to practice in Maryland, the rules of ethics don't allow us to advertise that we are "specialists" in any particular field of law, but we will be the first to tell you that we are not comfortable practicing all aspects of law. For example, we help people file for bankruptcy. We have for years. We don't help people with disputes over riparian rights. Don't know what that is? It's the law related to water rights (*e.g.*, what you can and can't do with a stream that runs through your property). There are attorneys who know that area of law well, but it's not us.

William has practiced bankruptcy law in three states and has focused practically his entire career on bankruptcy and the rights of debtors. Kelly is trained as a litigator and appellate advocate and has spent years learning bankruptcy strategy from William.

One Final Thought...

Don't be overwhelmed. We've had clients show up with boxes of unopened mail from years spent with their head in the sand. The longer they ignored their debt, the more overwhelmed they got. It just seemed like too big of a problem to tackle and, you know what, it probably was too big to handle alone.

We are here to help you.

We wrote this book to show you that there is hope. There are strategies that we can use to save your house, save your car, save your cash, save your marriage, and save your family. Our offices are filed with Holiday cards, baby announcements, and letters from clients who are so thankful to have their lives back. Nothing makes us happier than knowing that we helped a client and their family get back on track and find financial freedom.

***Even if you don't think we can help you,
call us anyway for some free advice.***

We've been in some tough spots before and we've helped a lot of clients. Let us be your sounding board. Who knows? Maybe we can help you see things in a new light. It might be as simple as helping you develop a budget or negotiate that one burdensome debt.

Once, the free advice that changed a client's life was simply to get rid of her car. She LOVED that car, but it was a lemon. By stopping those loan payments and repair costs, she was able to redirect her money to where she really needed it.

--Will

Every client and every financial situation is different. We don't know what will work for you until we talk. Tell us the truth, open up, let us know what is important to you, and we will work together to find the best solution for you and your family.

My 3-year old daughter asked me what I do for a living. I told her: "I'm a lawyer; I help people who are in trouble." That is my mission. No matter how it is that you got into financial trouble, whether it was a hurricane like me, a job loss like Kelly's father, or some wrong turns along the way, let us help you.
-Will

Before I met Will, I was a corporate attorney helping big companies deal with lawsuits. It was good work, but I never felt like I was helping anyone. Now, when I get a hug from a client or phone calls from clients just to say hello, I know I'm doing something good.
-Kelly

Grafton Firm

Protecting Families; Protecting Assets

(410) 870-9315
www.graftonfirm.com
www.mdbankruptcyfirm.com

Made in the USA
Monee, IL
14 September 2026

63198323R00046